Reb the Ram

By Cameron Macintosh

Reb the ram
sips at the pit.

Reb can see Rat
in the pit!

Sip, sip, sip!

Cat ran to the pit.

Rat can see Cat!

Rat sits at the tap.

Reb can see Cat.

Reb tips to Rat.

Rat ran!

Rat sits.

Cat sips at the pit.

Sip, sip, sip!

Rat is my pet!

CHECKING FOR MEANING

1. What animals are mentioned in the story? (*Literal*)

2. What does Rat do when Reb tips to him? (*Literal*)

3. Why is Rat referred to as Reb's pet? (*Inferential*)

EXTENDING VOCABULARY

pit	Look at the word *pit*. What does the word mean in this story?
Cat	Look at the word *Cat*. Can you think of other words that rhyme with *Cat*?
pet	Look at the word *pet*. What sounds are in this word? Which sound is changed to turn *pet* into *pat*?

MOVING BEYOND THE TEXT

1. How do you think Reb and Rat feel when they see each other at the pit?

2. How do you think Reb, Rat and Cat feel about each other? Why?

3. Can you relate this story to a real-life situation where two friends are separated and then reunited?

4. Why do you think the author chose to include a ram, a rat and a cat in the story?

SPEED SOUNDS

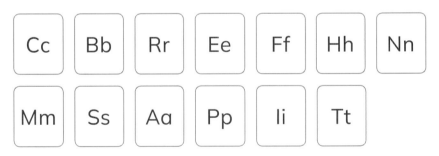

| Cc | Bb | Rr | Ee | Ff | Hh | Nn |

| Mm | Ss | Aa | Pp | Ii | Tt |

PRACTICE WORDS

ram

Reb

can

in

Rat

Cat

ran

pet